# Jane Addams

## SOCIAL REFORMER

### Darleen Ramos

Boston, Massachusetts
Chandler, Arizona
Glenview, Illinois
Upper Saddle River, New Jersey

**Illustrations**
5, 6, 9, 12 Meryl Treatner.

**Photographs**
Every effort has been made to secure permission and provide appropriate credit for photographic material.
The publisher deeply regrets any omission and pledges to correct errors called to its attention in subsequent editions.

Unless otherwise acknowledged, all photographs are the property of Pearson Education, Inc.

Photo locators denoted as follows: Top (T), Center (C), Bottom (B), Left (L), Right (R), Background (Bkgd)

Opener: Library of Congress; 1 Library of Congress; 2 Library of Congress; 3 Swarthmore College Peace Collection;
4 Library of Congress; 7 Detroit Publishing Company Photograph Collection/Library of Congress; 8 Library of Congress;
10 Swarthmore College Peace Collection; 11 Library of Congress; 13 Swarthmore College Peace Collection; 14 Library of
Congress; 15 Photos to Go/Photolibrary.

ISBN-13:  978-0-328-67619-4
ISBN-10:      0-328-67619-5

10 11 12 13 V0SI 18 17 16 15

# A Scene to Remember

It was a Saturday night in 1883. A group of Americans, touring London, England, came upon a crowd of poor people. It took the Americans a moment to realize the crowd was buying food. Every Saturday night this happened. Fruit and vegetable sellers would sell what hadn't been sold during the week. The food was often rotten. But that didn't bother the crowd. They were hungry and this was all they could afford. This food was better than no food at all.

Jane Addams was one of these tourists, and she never forgot what she saw. Later, Addams would dedicate her life to helping the poor in the United States. This is her story.

# Life in Cedarville

Jane Addams was born in the village of Cedarville, Illinois, on September 6, 1860. Her childhood was filled with both happiness and sadness.

Addams was only two when her mother died in childbirth. The result was that Addams and her father became even closer. Mr. Addams was one of the wealthiest men in Cedarville and he wanted his daughter to have a good life.

Addams was bright and cheerful. From an early age, she cared deeply about the problems of others. But she also had problems of her own. A childhood illness had left her with a curved spine. It caused terrible back pain. The result was that she felt ashamed about the way she looked. She sometimes described herself as an "Ugly Duckling."

# College and Medical School

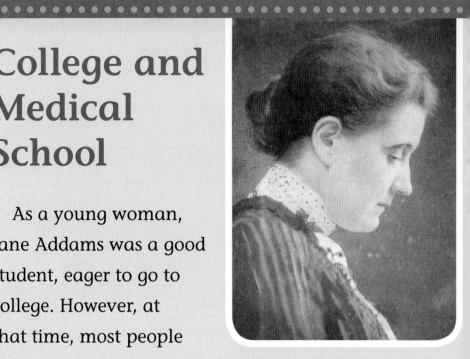

As a young woman, Jane Addams was a good student, eager to go to college. However, at that time, most people thought college was unnecessary for women. Few women attended college. But Addams was not interested in what others did or did not do. She applied to college anyway. Not surprisingly, this upset her father. To please him, Addams agreed to attend a local school for young women instead.

After graduating in 1881, Addams still had big dreams. She wanted to become a doctor. Once again, her father was not pleased. Hoping he could change her mind, he suggested they take a trip together. However, the trip ended sadly. Mr. Addams died. Now, Jane Addams felt lost.

After a period of mourning for her father, Addams decided to follow her dream. She began medical school and did very well. But her back pain got in the way. Finally, it became so severe that Addams had to leave school.

After months of suffering, Addams had back surgery. While she was recovering, her stepmother suggested a trip to Europe. Wealthy people often took long trips to learn new languages and tour historic sites. In 1883, Addams left home, eager for new adventures. It was in England that she saw poor people buying food.

# What Will I Do With My Life?

In 1885, Addams returned from her European tour. For the next few years, she helped care for a younger brother and sister. However, this was not very satisfying. Addams wanted a greater purpose for her life. If she wasn't going to be a doctor, what would she do?

Upon her father's death, Addams had **inherited** a large sum of money. Perhaps, she thought, she could use her wealth to help others.

## Important Places in Jane Addams's Life

Cedarville

● Chicago

**ILLINOIS**

# A New Idea

Still confused, Addams decided to return to Europe. Maybe, she thought, she would find her answer there. One day, it suddenly became clear to her. She was spending too much time worrying. It was time to stop talking about doing something. It was time to take action instead.

Ships like this one often took wealthy Americans to Europe.

Addams had a plan. She wanted to find a house in a poor neighborhood and provide help to those in need. She had heard about a similar place in London. It was run by a group of college students. They called the place a **settlement house**. The students lived in a poor neighborhood and worked to help the community in whatever way they could. Before she returned home, Addams visited them to get ideas about how to put her own plan into action.

# Chicago

Addams returned home, eager to start her own settlement house. Her good friend Ellen Starr would join Addams in Chicago.

The poor often lived in cramped quarters.

In 1889, Chicago was booming. As the numbers of factories increased, workers came to cities like Chicago. At the same time, **immigrants** from other countries arrived in search of freedom or a better life.

While Chicago offered plenty of opportunities, life was often very hard. Many newcomers didn't speak English. They often worked long hours for little pay. Families often crammed together into tiny apartments in **tenements**. The streets were often filthy and littered with garbage.

# Making a Start at Hull House

Addams and Starr found the perfect location in a neighborhood filled with immigrants. Settlement houses were new to the United States. Addams hoped hers would provide a place where poor people could find friendship and support. She hoped Hull House would help improve the community.

Once Hull House opened, neighbors wandered in. They wondered why two wealthy women would choose to live in such a neighborhood. Slowly, Addams and Starr began to earn the trust of their neighbors.

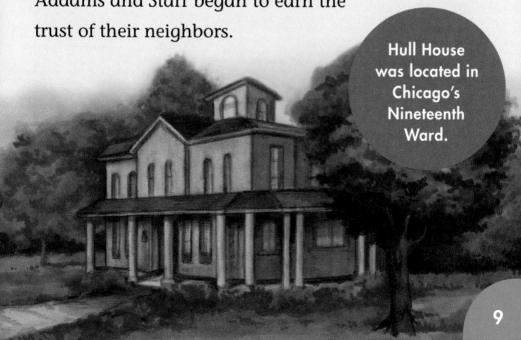

Hull House was located in Chicago's Nineteenth Ward.

# Helping Children

At first, Addams and Starr simply listened to their new neighbors. It was fortunate that Addams could speak and understand several languages. The visitors were happy to have someone to talk to and offer them comfort.

Hull House began to offer kindergarten classes and children's clubs. Now, working mothers had someone to look after their young children. And older children who had jobs could come after work to take classes and listen to stories.

Children played and read books at Hull House.

# Life on the Streets

Children in poor neighborhoods played in dirty streets.

In the late 1800s, life could be hard for children. Many often worked in the same factories as their parents. It was not unusual for older children to work 60 hours a week. And, without enough schools, children who didn't work were left to play in the streets.

Garbage was a big problem in many parts of Chicago. In poorer areas, it was rarely collected. The result was that children had to play alongside the piles of smelly, rotten trash. Many children became sick.

Addams complained to city hall and even offered to remove the trash herself. Instead, the mayor appointed Addams garbage **inspector**. She tried to clean up the neighborhood. No matter how much trash was removed, some streets were still covered with it.

# Sense of Community

Addams helped the older people in the community. Many of them felt alone because they did not speak English. Addams

An adult shows children how to make pottery.

brought together people of the same **culture** so that they could chat together. She helped create clubs for Greeks, Italians, Germans, and Russian Jewish groups to come together to sing, dance, and make friends.

Addams noticed that the children of immigrants were losing many of the **traditions** from their old countries. To change that, Addams invited immigrants to demonstrate their skills at Hull House. She even opened a museum to demonstrate crafts such as pottery making and weaving. In this way, she hoped to keep people's traditions alive.

# Hull House Grows

With the help of **volunteers**, as well as supporters who gave money, Addams and Starr expanded the settlement house. Hull House now had a library, a kindergarten, and a gym. For the first time, neighborhood children had a playground.

By 1907, Hull House was no longer a single building. It consisted of 13 buildings and covered a city block! Neighbors had much to enjoy. There were activities that taught them skills and brightened their days. Addams organized reading groups, art classes, and a theater. Eventually, there was even a swimming pool.

# Speaking Out for Peace

In 1914, World War I had begun in Europe. Addams was a **pacifist**. She did not believe in war. She felt strongly that conflicts between countries could be solved peacefully. Although the United States had not yet entered the war, Addams wanted to make sure it would not. She became the leader of the Women's Peace Party and spoke out for peace. Some criticized her for her opinions.

During the 1920s, Addams traveled around the world speaking out for peace. A heart attack finally forced her to return home to Chicago. In 1931, she received the Nobel Peace Prize. She was the first woman to be so honored.

# Neighbors Helping Neighbors

Jane Addams spent her last years watching Hull House continue to grow. She died on May 21, 1935, at the age of 74.

Thousands of people attended her funeral at Hull House. She was buried in Cedarville near her mother and father.

Today, Addams's ideas still live on in Chicago and around the world. The Jane Addams Hull House Association has several community centers. They offer childcare, classes, and support to more than 60,000 people a year. And, because of the work Addams began, settlement houses and centers around the country provide help to communities. Addams would be pleased to see that neighbors are still helping neighbors.

# Glossary

**culture** a way of life shared by a group of people

**immigrant** a person who settles in a new country

**inherit** to receive from someone who dies

**inspector** someone who has the job of checking something carefully

**pacifist** someone who is opposed to war as a solution to conflicts

**settlement house** a place that provides help and services for those in need

**tenement** a building that was divided into many very small apartments

**tradition** a custom, or way of doing something, that has been handed down over time

**volunteer** someone who offers to do work to help people, without asking for pay